# A Tennessee Tune

by KAYE PELTIER

Selah Press PUBLISHING

A Tennessee Tune by Kaye Peltier

Song Writer: Kaye Peltier
Managing Editor: Kayla Fioravanti

**Cover Design:** Kayla Fioravanti
**Front Cover Photo**: Kayce Williams
**Back Cover Photos:** Kayce Williams, Nancy Carter Ranchino, Paul D. Cookson, and Franklin Farmers Market

ISBN-13: 978-0692801383 (Selah Press)
ISBN-10:0692801383

Copyright © 2016 Kaye Peltier
Printed in the United States of America
Published by Selah Press, LLC

# Dedication

This book is dedicated to my husband, Bruce. For 45 years you have been my life's mate, my best friend, my partner and spiritual leader. To me, this makes up my whole world. I love you.

Download audio at PeltierBooksandMusic.com

**I start the day with a Tennessee sunrise**

**and the tune of a Mockingbird's song**

*Mockingbird is the Tennessee state bird.

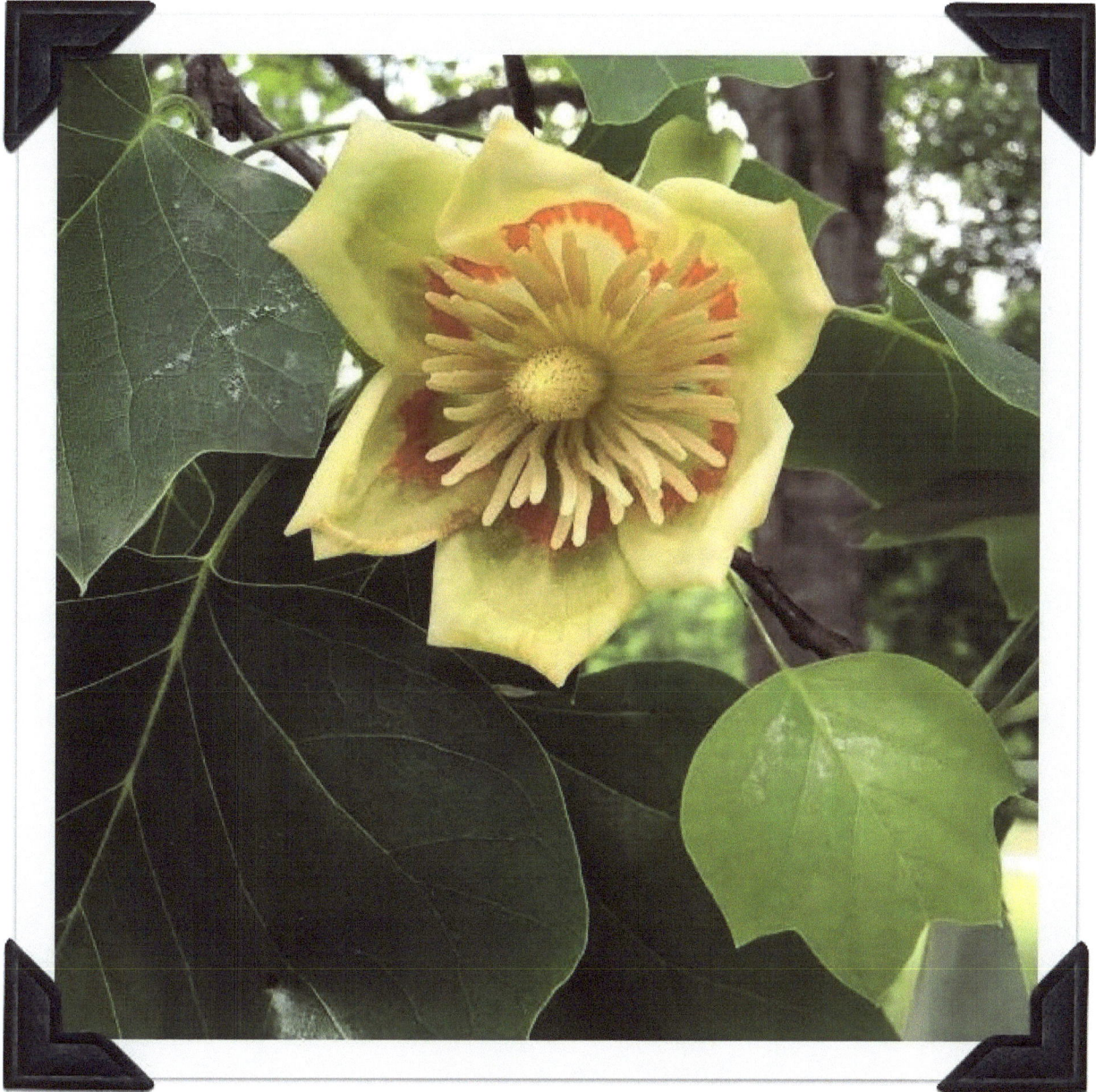

# who sits high on the Tulip Poplar

*Tulip Poplar is the Tennessee state tree.

## till his sound falls to Tennessee ground

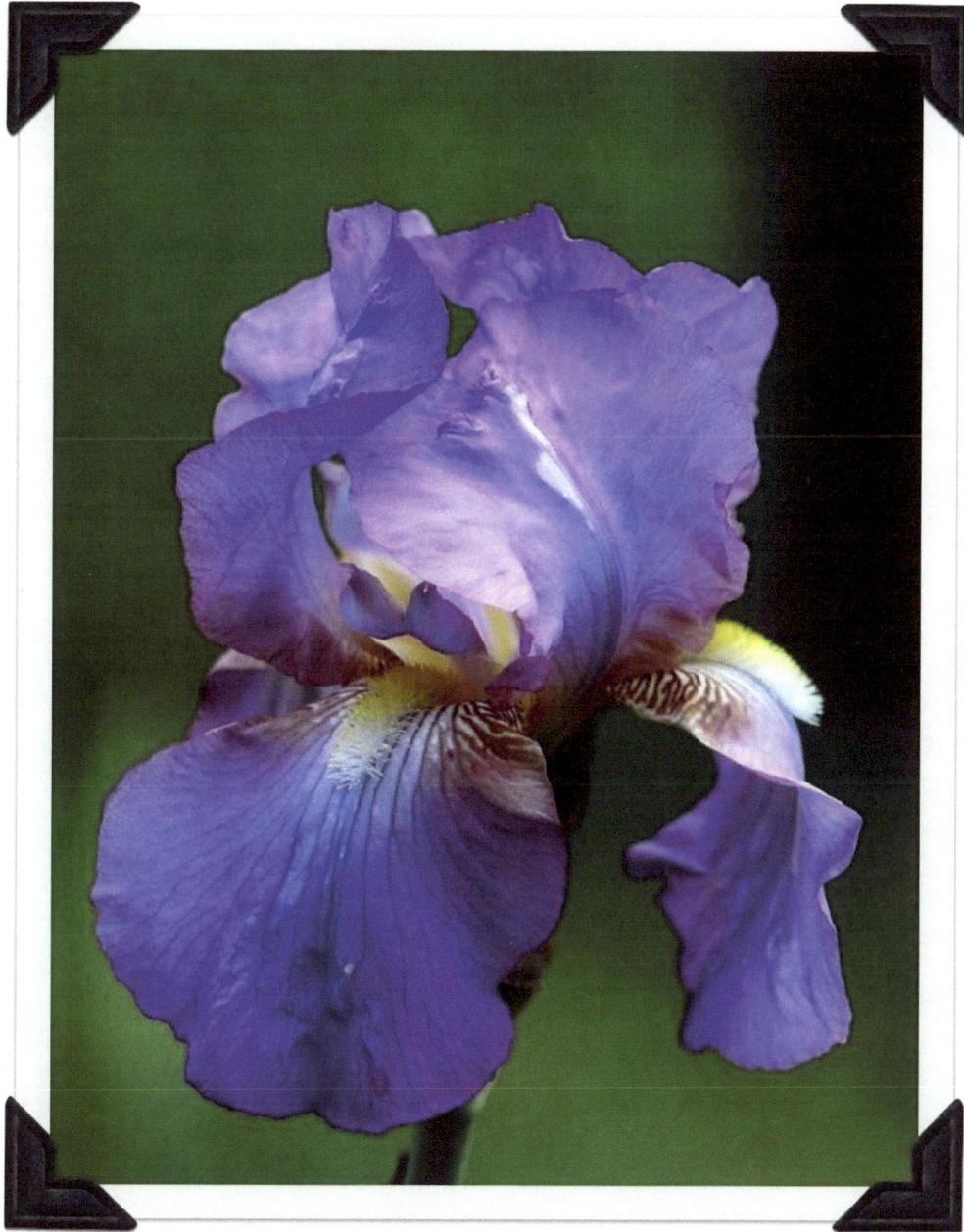

## at the site of the first purple iris

*Iris is the Tennessee state flower.

**and the wildflowers all in bloom**

## a garden full of juicy tomatoes

*Tomato is the Tennessee state fruit.

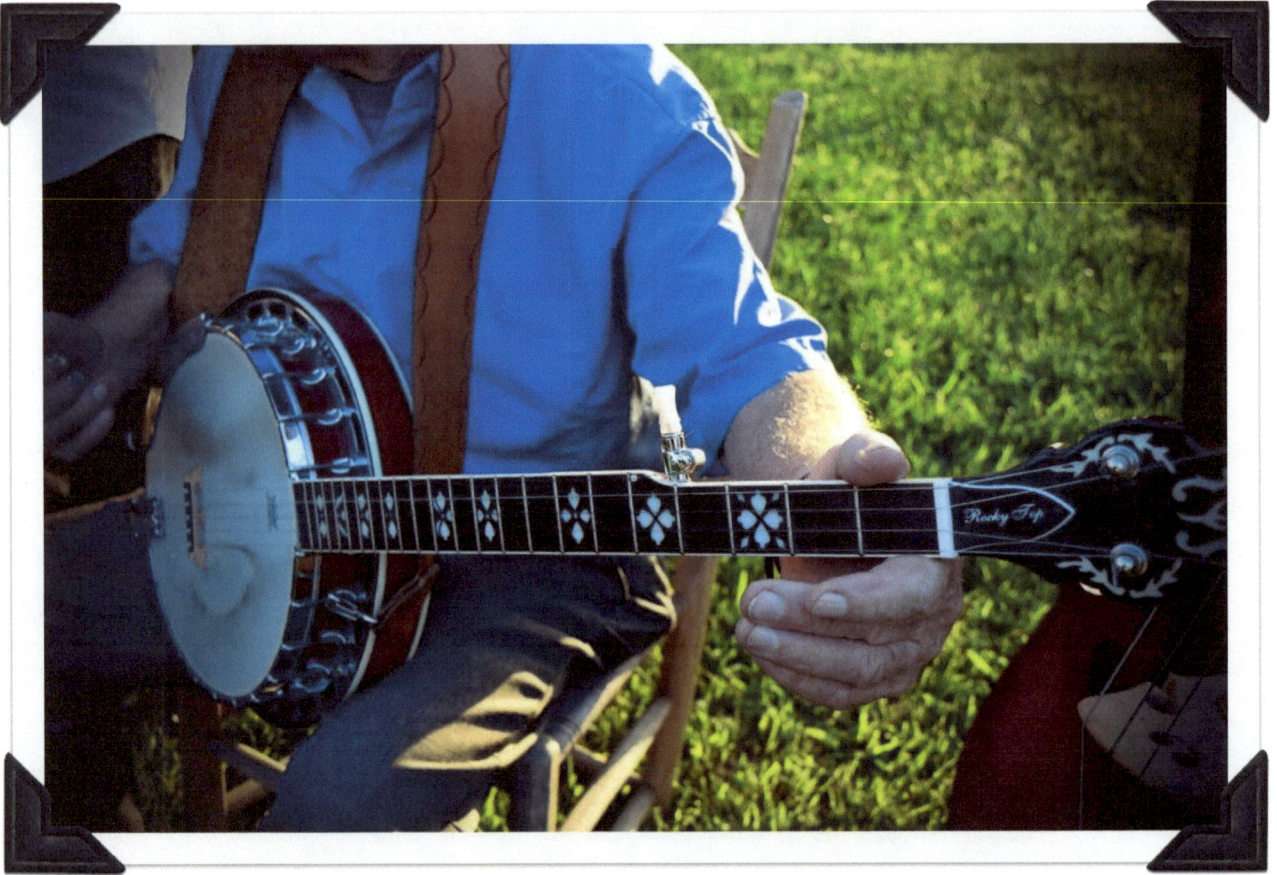

**now all I need is a Tennessee tune.**

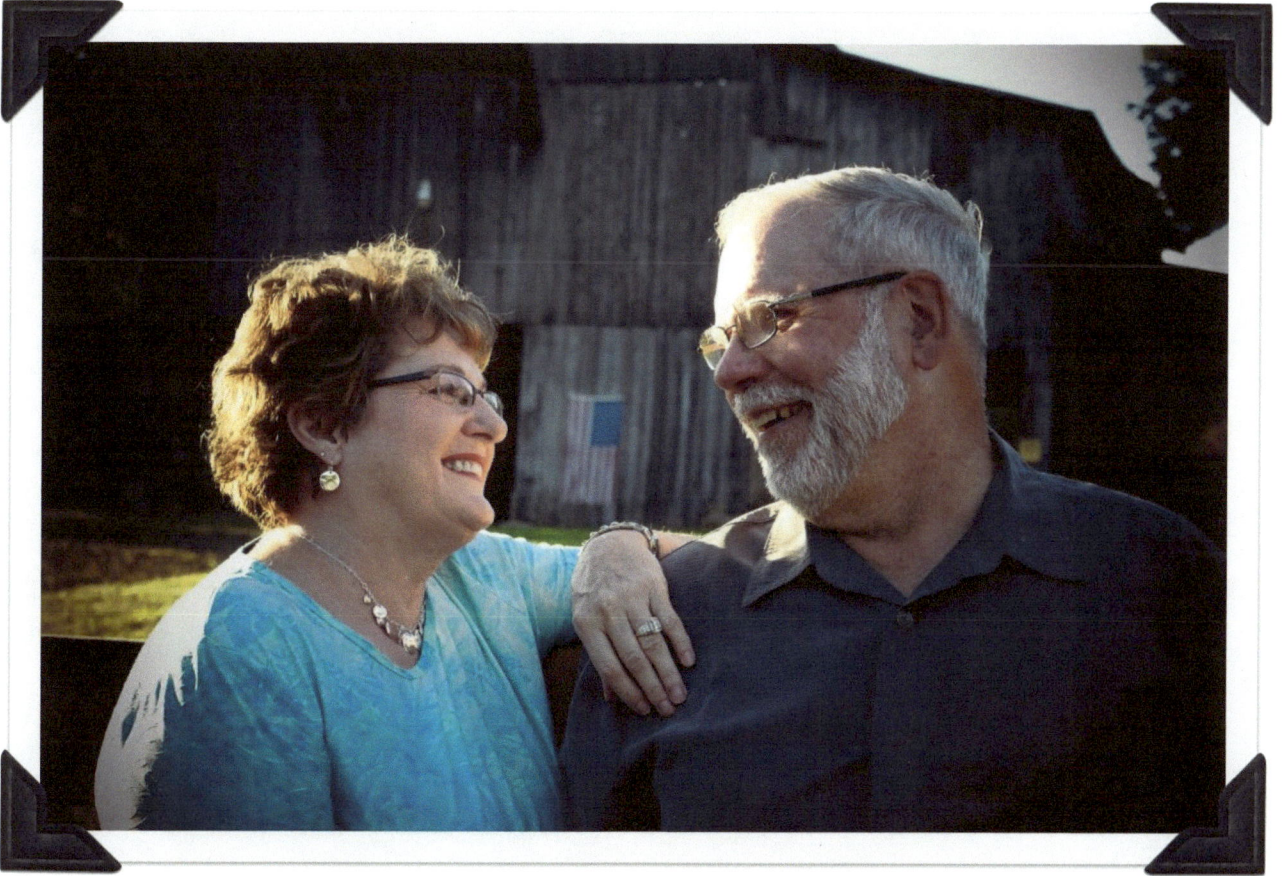

# A Tennessee tune; about good times and bad

**comes straight from the heart
some happy, some sad.**

**But a Tennessee tune is a gift from above.**

**I'll have a great afternoon
with a Tennessee tune.**

# Down by the stream lives a big box turtle

*Box turtle is the Tennessee state reptile.

**and a raccoon family too.**

*Raccoon is the Tennessee state wild animal.

## **Ladybugs and swallowtail butterflies**

*Ladybug is the Tennessee state insect.

**all saying how-do-you-do.**

*Swallowtail is the Tennessee state butterfly.

# Hope I find the catfish a bitin'
# I'll wet me a line or two

*Catfish is the Tennessee state fish.

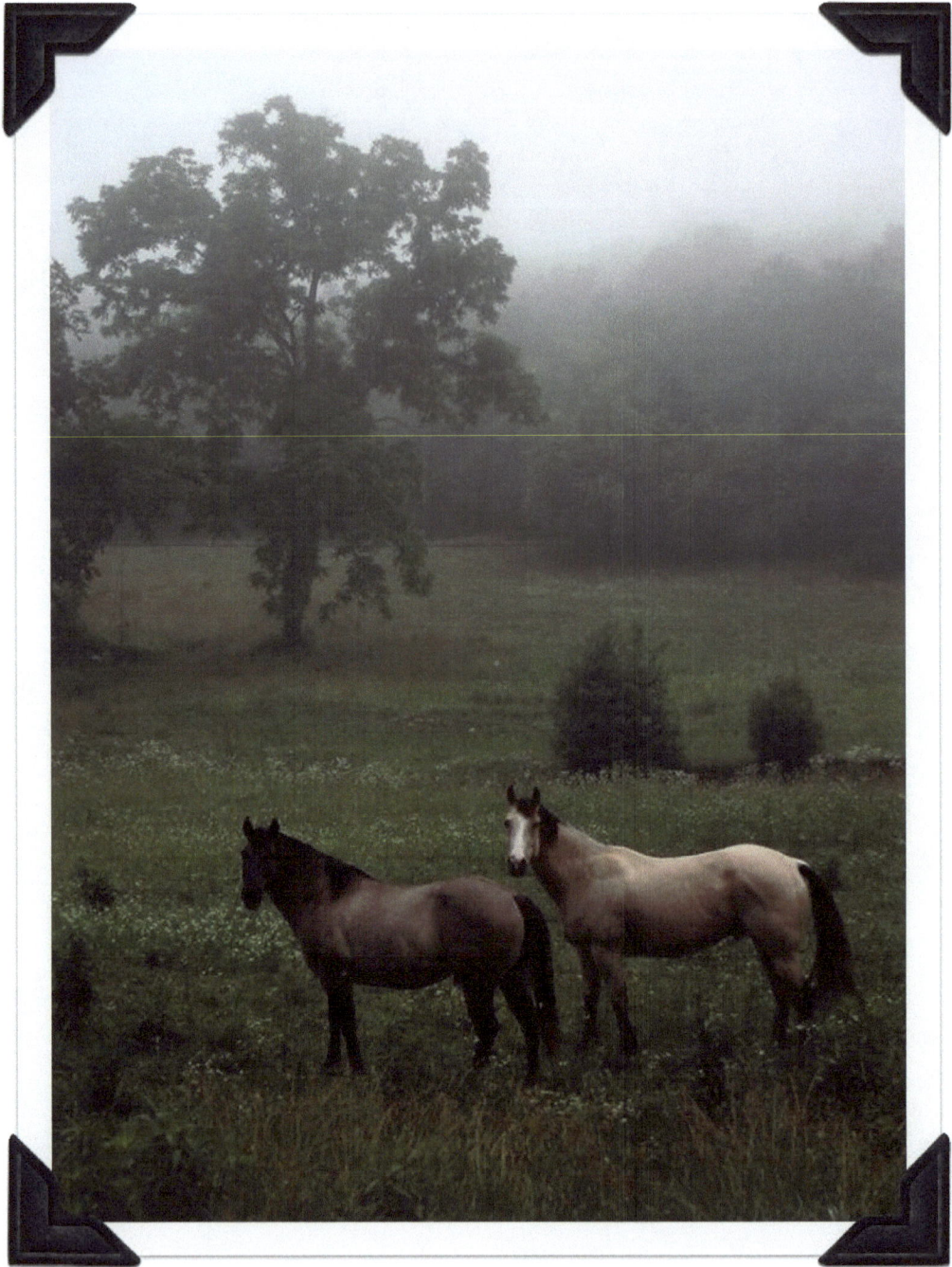

**with all the beauty that's around me
think I'll write another Tennessee tune.**

# A Tennessee tune;
# about good times and bad

**comes straight from my heart
some happy, some sad.**

\* Tennessee state flag.

**But this Tennessee tune
is a gift from above**

**and I'll be finished real soon
with my Tennessee tune.**

**I am blessed with close family around me**

**and I enjoy my church going friends**

**and the sounds of Sunday go-to-meetin' singing songs with a Tennessee blend.**

**Then once again on the porch at evenin'
the singers and pickers get tuned**

**and as the sun sets softly behind us
we'll end the day with a Tennessee tune.**

# A Tennessee tune;
# about good times and bad

**comes straight from the heart
some happy, some sad.**

## But a Tennessee tune
## is a gift from above

**And sittin' under the moon we're singing Tennessee tunes, here under the moon singing a Tennessee tune.**

# Tennessee *Symbols*

## A TENNESSEE TUNE

by Kaye Peltier

85 G       F   C   89 G   F   G7   93

Tennesee tune about     good times and bad   comes straight from theheart some happy some sad.   But a

C              C7 97 F          C    10 G7

Tennessee tune   is a   gift from a------ bove----   I'll be finished real soon   with my   Tennessee

C        105        109       G

tune.   I am blessed with   close family around me   and I en----joy my   church going friends

113            117       C

and the sounds of Sun-daygo-to ---meetin'   singing songs with a   Tennessee blend.   Then once a-

121            C7   125       F

gain on   the porch at   evenin'--   The singers and pickers   get   tuned   and as

129       C       G7   133       C

the sun sets   softly be   hind----------- us   we'll end the day with a   Tennessee tune.   A

G7   137       F   C   G7   141

Tennessee------- tune about good times and bad   comes straight from the heart some happy some sad   but a

145 C       C7   F 149       C       G7

Tennessee tune   is a   gift from a------bove   And sittin' under the moon   we're singing a Tennessee

153 CF       C       G7   157 C

tune, here under   the   moon   singing   a Ten-ne----ss--ee tune.

# About
## the Author

Kaye Peltier has been playing the piano and singing since she was 10 yrs. old. As a teenager she traveled with her brother and twin sister all over the USA performing in concerts and church services. The Ferguson Trio recorded three albums together. Two years after her marriage to Bruce Peltier, she got off the road and began a family. Her daughter, Kayce was born and she continued to minister in local churches as soloist, choir director and pianist.

When her grandson was born she began writing songs for children to "help Tanner learn the Bible and how Jesus loved him," Kaye said. She also was requested to write for Vacation Bible School and she began to write more children's songs as well as Praise and Worship songs. These songs were used as she was Worship leader in three churches in the Nashville area. While her husband was pastoring a church in Columbia, Kaye felt led to start a community choir. "There were many smaller churches in our area that did not have enough people to have their own choir". Kaye used people from churches all around to form a choir that could do concerts, community Christmas programs and worship services. "We worked for five years and saw God work among not only the choir members and myself, but those in the community."

When Kaye's mother became sick Kaye left church music service to be her mother's caregiver. During the first two years, Kaye went back to school and became a Certified Music Practitioner. "My mother was the one who taught me to sing so I wanted to give back to her with healing music." Bruce and Kaye decided to take one of the songs she had written into a children's book called *Fruit of the Spirit* which comes with a download of her song of the same name. Kaye's music on her CDs *Safe and Secure* and *Shared Moments* are filled with healing music. She has done speaking engagements in local schools to share about book writing and the love of Jesus. "God has so blessed me by music. I plan on serving Him for the rest of my life sharing and caring for those He so loves."

# About
## the Photographers

**Megan Blackwell** lives in North Mississippi with her husband Stephen and their five children. She spends most of her free time with her family and friends making memories whether it be vacations at the beach or a Sunday dinner. Megan is passionate about capturing her children's lives in photos. When not managing a successful dental practice she enjoys traveling, riding motorcycles, and crafts.

**Paul D. Cookson** was born and raised in San Antonio TX. He has been photographing beautiful landscapes and other subjects for the last 15 years. Paul is also an international author and a percussionist. He and his wife and daughter currently live in Spring Hill, TN.

**Dana Lynne** loves to write, sing, take pretty pictures and is a true southern belle. Her ultimate goal is to glorify her heavenly Father by using the gifts He has placed inside her. She is thankful for opportunities like this to give a platform to the beauty she has witnessed. She hopes to influence and inspire others for good. You can read her blog at Danalyne.wordpress.com.

**Charles Marsh** is retired and lives along the beautiful Natchez Trace Parkway in Williamson County, Franklin, TN. He enjoys photography as a hobby and loves to photograph butterflies, hummingbirds, wildlife and the scenery along the Natchez Trace Parkway.

**Nancy Carter Ranchino** is a middle TN native that loves capturing the simple beauty of the hills and hollows where she grew up and still lives today. Along with photography, she enjoys reading, sewing, crafting and hiking to waterfalls. When life gets overwhelming, a little 'nature therapy' is her favorite remedy. The heavens declare the glory of God; the skies proclaim the work of his hands. Psalms 19:1

**Lisa Rodgers** is a natural light photographer, she lives in the south, and she uses the word y'all...**a lot**! Lisa loves candid, not posed. Flowing, not stiff. She shoots pictures based on the life that surrounds her clients. In addition to people, she shoots animals, landscape, architect, products and more. In a nutshell....she captures life! Spending time with family and friends is what Lisa loves the most. In her spare time, you will likely find her on their volleyball court or simply relaxing in the country surrounded by 27 fuzzy paper weights {aka cats}, and the love of her life, her husband Prevo. Shoot Y'all Photography is a about a southern gal capturing life, and its natural surroundings.

**Kayce Williams** Is a lifelong Tennessean. She was raised in Franklin, Tennessee where she met and married her husband and started her family. After the birth of her son in 1999, they moved a few miles south to Spring Hill, Tennessee where they still reside today. At the age of 4 Kayce was diagnosed with a genetic disorder commonly known as O.S.S. Ooo Shiny Syndrome is incurable and treatments can be very expensive, but she is committed to managing it fervently. She will have to undergo retail therapy for the rest of her life, but maintains an upbeat disposition that living a full life with this disorder is not only attainable, but vital. Kayce is devoted to family, strong in her faith, has an abundance of creative energy, and is passionate about people and public service to her community.

**The Franklin Farmers Market** is a true Tennessee farmers market. It's Tennessee farm fresh food from real farmers and a select number of local craft persons, every Saturday morning at the Franklin Farmers Market. The non-profit Franklin Farmers Market believes that local family farms can remain successful with support from the market to stay productive. Productive family farms are important to both the economic and environmental structures of Middle Tennessee communities and the Franklin Farmers Market is working to ensure the future of farming in Tennessee.